and
Green Kni...

Tony Mitton
Illustrated by Arthur Robins

ORCHARD BOOKS

CRAZY CAMELOT

MEET THE KNIGHTS OF THE ROUND TABLE:

King Arthur
with his sword so bright,

Sir Percival,
a wily knight.

Sir Kay,
a chap whose hopes are high,

Sir Lancelot,
makes ladies sigh.

Sir Gawain,
feeling rather green,

Sir Galahad,
so young and keen.

Sir Ack,
who's fond of eating lots,

Sir Mordred,
hatching horrid plots.

Morgana,
Arthur's wicked
sister,

Merlin.
That's me,
your wizard mister!

To Bold Sir Bernard Mitton, Order of the Knights of the Colander, and the Lady Clare, from Scribe Tony

To Sir Hayden Thomas Skerry, from Arthur Robins

ORCHARD BOOKS
96 Leonard Street, London EC2A 4XD
Orchard Books Australia
32/45-51 Huntley Street, Alexandria, NSW 2015
First published in Great Britain in 2003
First paperback edition 2004
Text © Tony Mitton 2003
Illustrations © Arthur Robins 2003
The rights of Tony Mitton to be identified as the author
and Arthur Robins as the illustrator of this work
have been asserted by them in accordance with the
Copyright, Designs, and Patents Act, 1988.
A CIP catalogue record for this book is available
from the British Library.
ISBN 1 84121 724 7 (hardback)
ISBN 1 84121 726 3 (paperback)
1 3 5 7 9 10 8 6 4 2 (hardback)
1 3 5 7 9 10 8 6 4 2 (paperback)
Printed in Great Britain

Back in the Middle Ages,
when men wore metal gear,
there lived a bunch of nutty knights
who seemed to show no fear.

They clanked around on horses
and looked for things to do.
They fought with fiery dragons
and spooky creatures too.

King Arthur ruled these nutty knights
at Crazy Camelot.
The castle was quite cosy
and the stew was always hot.

I am the wizard Merlin.
My beard is long and white.
My busy brain is full of tales
to fill you with delight.

I'll gaze into my crystal ball
to help me think of one...
Aha! The tale of young Gawain -
I think you'll find this fun.

It all begins at Christmas,
that special time of year,
when people put on parties
and folk are full of cheer.

King Arthur's Christmas parties
were said to be just great,
with dancing, games and presents,
and goodies on your plate.

The guests were met. The feast was set.
The folk were in the Hall.
"It's Christmas!" cried King Arthur.
"So let's begin our ball.

"We'll start with funky dancing.
So, come on. Take the floor—"
But suddenly a heavy pounding
shook the great oak door.

The knocking seemed to fill the air.
Everybody stopped.
Then, as the door swung open,
aghast, all jaws just dropped.

For in there rode a massive man,
as big as ever seen.
But what was most peculiar -
the bloke was glowing green!

His hair was green, his skin was green,
his clothes were green, of course.
And just to match the rest of him,
he rode a dark green horse.

The Green Knight glanced about
  the Hall.
"Is this King Arthur's place?
Are these his famous fearless knights?"
He looked from face to face.

"Why, yes," spoke up King Arthur.
"You've crashed our Christmas feast.
So, why not join the party?
Or have a drink, at least…"

"No thanks," the Green Knight
    answered him.
"I've come to set a test.
Now, who will dare to challenge me?
Which knight round here is best?"

Well, normally, each eager knight
would leap to take the task.
But as this guy was huge and green,
they weren't so keen to ask.

"And is this really Camelot?"
the Green Knight cried out loud.

I'd heard you lot were really hot.
What a weedy crowd!

18

"Enough!" called young Sir Gawain.

Greeny, I'm your man.
I'll take your test and do my best.
Scare me - if you can!

The Green Knight turned to Gawain.
"So you're prepared to try.
The rules are these," he stated,
a twinkle in his eye.

"You have to hit me with my axe
just here, where I show.
Then visit me this time next year,
and I'll return the blow."

"This bloke is barmy," Gawain thought.
"He's pointing to his neck.
He'll lose his head then he'll be dead...
Perhaps I'd better check."

"I can't just slice your head off,"
he said. "That won't be fair."
The Green Knight knelt and
answered back,

Chicken. Don't you dare?

Sir Gawain thought, "I'm stuck with this.
Too late to back down now."
"OK, green guy. It's time to die:
Steady... Aim..."

The Green Knight's head went
   whizzing off
and tumbled to the ground.
Some people gasped. Some people
   groaned.
And some just gulped and frowned.

But did the Green Knight crumple?
No, up he got instead.
He calmly strode across the hall
and lifted high his head.

He held it by its long green hair.
The face began to sneer.

You'll find me by the Chapel Green,
I'll see you there next year.

With that he jumped upon his horse
and rode into the night.
And when he'd gone the folk said,
   "Phew!"
And shut the door up tight.

"Let's not forget it's Christmas,"
said Gawain with a grin.
"Indeed!" cried out King Arthur.
"Let the feast begin."

But while the feast went gaily on
Gawain began to brood.
The thought of what awaited him
had put him off his food.

I'll have to face that fiend again.
I'll have to feel his blade.
A noble knight should not feel fright.
But, blimey – I'm afraid!

Too soon the year had turned around
and it was time to go.
So Gawain wended wearily
through wind and rain and snow.

Yes, north he travelled, far he rode,
to find the Chapel Green.
The way was tough, the weather rough.
Gawain grew worn and lean.

He fought with dragons, monsters, trolls.
He fought with brigand bands.
And when his weapons didn't work
he fought them with bare hands.

But deep inside himself he had
the very biggest fight.
He had to force himself to find
that gruesome great Green Knight.

And, just when he was thinking
that searching was in vain,
he came across a castle
upon a sweet, green plain.

The kindly knight who lived there
said, "Come inside and stay.
The Chapel Green's not far from here.
I'll help you on your way.

"But you look cold and chilly,
and rather tired, I fear.
Rest up with me till morning.
You'll be much cosier here."

So Gawain took his armour off.
Oh, see how he'd grown thinner.
He sat down by a warming fire
and ate a splendid dinner.

He told the knight his story.
Then, rested, warm and fed,
he grew all tired and snorey
and toddled off to bed.

The next day was the day he meant
to meet the great Green Knight.
But when it came to breakfast time,
his tummy felt all tight.

His host said, "Why not stay in bed?
You really don't look well.
Just say you couldn't find him.
Trust me - I won't tell.

"Who wants to have their head
   chopped off?
Perhaps you needn't go.
It makes more sense to chicken out.
And no one needs to know."

"Oh, sir," said good Sir Gawain,
"you seem a noble knight.
To lie and cheat and miss the meet -
you can't pretend that's right."

His kind host shrugged, then
    wished him luck
and pointed out the way.
He said to reach the Chapel
would take just half a day.

And when Gawain arrived there,
at that place of greeny shade,
he heard the sound of sharpening,
a grindstone on a blade.

The great Green Knight came
    striding up,
"What!? No shakes or fear?
I didn't think you'd dare to show.
Well done. You've come. You're here."

Gawain, he knelt and waited.
But, as the blade came down
he flinched - and so the
   Green Knight stopped
and gave Gawain a frown.

"What? Gone and lost your bottle?
A knight from Camelot?"
"OK," Gawain said, "this time
I will not flinch a jot!"

A second time the blade flew down.
It gave his neck a tickle.
A blob of blood came dribbling out,
but really, just a trickle...

"You've had your go!" cried Gawain.
"So now, put down your axe."
"Don't worry," smiled the Green Knight.
"You've proved yourself. Relax."

The Green Knight started melting
as if he were a ghost,
till underneath Sir Gawain saw
his kindly smiling host.

"It's you!" cried out Sir Gawain.
"Aha! I might have guessed.
You told me I should chicken out
just so I'd fail the test."

"Indeed," his host said, smiling.
"But how it pleases me
to find that you are brave and true
and full of chivalry.

"I thought King Arthur's knights
    were wimps,
but clearly, I was wrong.
King Arthur's guys deserve a prize!
From now on that's my song!"

When bold Sir Gawain got back home,
they brought out cakes and ale,
and huddled round a roaring fire
to hear him tell his tale.

So this is Merlin signing off.
Just watch this trick. It's mean!
I shriek KAZOOO! Then grow into
a dragon! Aren't I green?

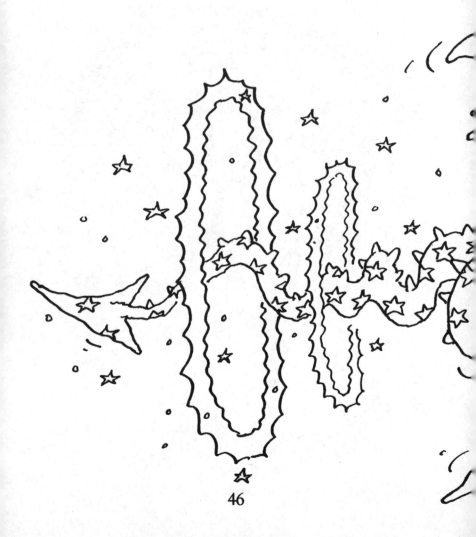

CRAZY CAMELOT CAPERS

Written by Tony Mitton
Illustrated by Arthur Robins

KING ARTHUR AND THE MIGHTY CONTEST
ISBN 1 84121 714 X   £3.99

EXCALIBUR THE MAGIC SWORD
ISBN 1 84121 718 2   £3.99

SIR LANCELOT AND THE BLACK KNIGHT
ISBN 1 84121 722 0   £3.99

SIR GAWAIN AND THE GREEN KNIGHT
ISBN 1 84121 726 3   £3.99

SIR GALAHAD AND THE GRAIL
ISBN 1 84362 001 4   £3.99

MORGANA THE SPOOKY SORCERESS
ISBN 1 84362 002 2   £3.99

BIG SIR B AND THE MONSTER MAID
ISBN 1 84362 003 0   £3.99

MEAN MORDRED AND THE FINAL BATTLE
ISBN 1 84362 004 9   £3.99

Crazy Camelot Capers are available from all good bookshops,
or can be ordered direct from the publisher:
Orchard Books, PO BOX 29, Douglas IM99 1BQ
Credit card orders please telephone 01624 836000
or fax 01624 837033
or e-mail: bookshop@enterprise.net for details.

To order please quote title, author and ISBN
and your full name and address.
Cheques and postal orders should be
made payable to 'Bookpost plc'.
Postage and packing is FREE within the UK
(overseas customers should add £1.00 per book).

Prices and availability are subject to change.